PASSION OF ST. GANGOLF

Hrotsvita of Gandersheim

Translated by: D.P. Curtin

Dalcassian Publishing Company

PHILADELPHIA, PA

Copyright @ 2005 Dalcassian Publishing Company

All rights reserved. No part of this publication may be reproduced, distributed, or transmitted in any form or by any means, including photocopying, recording, or other electronic or mechanical methods, without the prior written permission of the publisher, except in the case of brief quotations embodied in critical reviews and certain other non-commercial uses permitted by copyright law. For permission request, write to Dalcassian Publishing Company at dalcassianpublishing at gmail.com

ISBN: 979-8-8692-3775-0 (Paperback)

Library of Congress Control Number:
Author: Curtin, D.P. (1985-)

Printed by Ingram Content Group, 1 Ingram Blvd, La Vergne, Tennessee

First printing edition 2005.

PASSION OF ST. GANGOLF

LIFE OF GANGOLF.

Gangolf, born of the noble family and blood of the Burgundian kings, and initiated into the Christian religion, had bought from a poor peasant a garden with a very pleasant fountain, the charm of which Hroswitha describes most beautifully. Into this garden, for the grace of prayer and relaxation, while he was free from arms and the republic, he was wont to admit, a thing which his relatives vehemently hated. It happened, then, that the spring had dried up, which he, having fixed in the ground with a stick, restored again with the most abundant stream, so that the wave of that wave drove away the plagues of all diseases, which draw and wash away. At last, marrying a wife who had been intemperate and unchastised, and in the love of her attendants, indulged in unbridled lust; that she had been found with the holy man, Gangolf, he rebuked her for her incontinence, she laid an ambush for Gangolf by her companions, and was killed by them, buried in a place called Nilland, famous for miracles. The fact that it had been related to Ganea, his wife, derogates from the belief in his miracles, and he considers miracles to be nothing but the rumbling of his own belly. Wherefore, as long as he lived, his belly was perpetually creaking in treachery of punishment.

PREFACE TO GANGOLF.

O pious Illuminator, Creator of the world and of things,
Who paints the sky with various stars,
Alone and reigning astrigas reigning in the court of
Light, holding all things, and ruling by rule,
You who through your own ages made the Born,
And the triune machine of things from nothing,
Who was the protoplast, rightly from the earth created,
to the nectar of the mouth of the divine, namely, your
sense of life, perhaps you breathed the liquid,
so that the fixed finger becomes the work of
your own, You deign to pour out your hungry hearts,
Hrosvitha, roaring piety,
with a song that I can control to fill the pious deeds of
St. Gangolf, the excellent martyr,
And to praise you always blessed name,
who after wars you will give to your servants welcome
rewards, transparent and thin for the wound of life,
commanding to live in the kingdom of light.

THE PASSION OF ST. GANGOLF THE MARTYR

At the time when Pepin the First held
the royal scepter of the Franks for the people, and
ruled the kingdoms of Burgundy with a magnificent law,
His subjects were duly tamed by his bridles,
A famous young man was nourished in those parts,
Mighty in arms, conspicuous in body,
By the name of Gangolf, charming by the honesty of his manners,
He was dear to all; he stood still and calm.
They say that he arose from the offspring of kings,
and was royal by his excellent manners.
His hope hangs from his mother's bosom in him,
Who created all things out of nothing by word,
He does not believe himself to be a germ and such an honor,
But passes through the merits of the lineage of his race.
For the benevolent mother, blessed with such a fetus,
sheds the light of the world as this child,
He quickly washes away the sins of the old with baptism,
Which protoplasts the fathers obtain, With
the ointment of Chrism written on his forehead and the sign,
He is born of the bright Church,
He is nourished and full of faith soon with the doctrine of the three,
While he wanders, cradle the milky body.
As often as he sucked milk, as often he took the sacraments of faith,
Suspended on the mother's twin breasts.
He slept with such, milked while he lived on the gurgling,
From here he pulsated, with his pregnant wit,
And the gray hair of his old limbs meditating with his fingers,
He does not infrequently spend his time in sacred studies.
Whom soon the beardless man, growing in all honesty,
The grace of Pippin, the prince of the almighty,
The royal court orders not undeservedly to stand,
Ardently worshiping such a young man with a heart.
But his piety, though the most just of a king,
would enrich him with so many glorious gifts,
a king who had been the first proconsul for years,
yet he was not raised to the pride of Turgent;

For the census of his country had been given to him most of all,
and he distributed it with such zeal to the poor,
that he might feel Christ wretched among the needy.
Oft Job, and blessed by the rule of men, He himself had a sick hand, a foot, and the gout;
Nor did he perspire for human reasons,
making himself equal to the first masters.
For, badly if our ears had pretended, Old age
had not played with false things and doubts,
Here, whom our hands have already begun to
paint as a saint, He is
accustomed to follow the four-footed path.
to give up the victory,
When the iron wedges are forged,
He himself always raises his triumph but from the enemy,
Safe with the help of the divine heavens.
Certainly not ours can
weave dactylic modules by dictating Camena's composition,
How many beloved signs had varied this
King of kings, supreme for his goodness.
But still, however uncultivated in speech, I will bark
One of the most famous and diverse.
As the facts proved, he led the troops,
captured the people sufficiently swollen by Mars,
stood up and as usual the victor soon ended the war,
his crimson blood unscathed,
the nations hostile to the law and subject to his own,
signed the census, peace was given, and returned.
He happened to go along the road, opposite to
each other's fence,
where he hid a small house painted with vernal flowers, roofed
with many shoots and hairs.
Hither, where the illustrious elder led the birds,
Perusing the liquid stream of the
spring, For a little while seized by the coldness of the lymph,
He halted, and, at his request, slows down his journey,
And sending the boy, he begged that
Florigeri, lord of that place, should come to him.
He who fulfills the commandments of the commander at the same time,
when he had been ordered, goes out more quickly.
Indeed, while the leader himself looked at this person coming,
he attacked directly with flattering addresses,
and beseeching him with all the sweetness of his mind,

he formed such words with his tongue:
Sweet friend, I beg you to be generous to my prayers,
that you may sell me this pure fountain,
which, clear from glasses and sweet with the sound of the waves,
This field, flowing down, irrigates this field and yours, And
soon I will generously pour out no small sums
of silver for your approved reward .
But when, giving a tinkling sound, the happy promise
passes through the ears of the person in small ones,
the face is happy, all the veins also fly,
in the secret of the heart that hides instead.
Then the poor man began to break out in such a voice.
Beyond what you believe, knowing hope and doubt,
O worthy of ours, second to none in piety,
Whom Eous worships in mind, in faith, the people,
Who for you, what can you make worthy of my tongue?
Is not our salvation in your hands?
And whatever you have to do for me by the word of your sanction,
although it is quite difficult and burdensome,
yet it is fair for me to submit to you, blessed one,
as for a while I am a little lord of the highest.
If it pleases me, an old man, to migrate from here,
I will not fight back, but I will follow your orders.
He says these things, and presses his words to his lips.
And against the king's piety,
He received such words from those who were playing, for his goodness,
And sooner than said, he paid the promises to the poor man,
Attributing to him hundreds of solids.
When he had finished these things, he returned with haste, and
endeavored to go on to the country he had inhabited.
Then those who had not been acquainted with the sign of veneration,
were about to do what Altithronus once was,
began to blaspheme the leader in silent whispers,
and to slander the work of piety or deed.
Believing that the man of piety had not hid the trick,
But soon the clandestine words spoken to him would be exposed.
He who gave a loud voice then to the palate, and
with these words he addresses his comrades,
Why do I wish, O comrades, to rebuke you, my dear ones, with
more than just words that are quite illegal for me?
The cause of their folly, saying that they had given me
money to an unknown man and a stranger,
I was empty of so much grief and merit,

and well-traded by me as a spring,
the right hand or my own tax, which is generous with piety,
if I gave gold for gifts to the smallest.
This is not befitting our opener bears,
What does the addict want for the sake of his value,
But he promises to settle your agitated
minds. The liquid stream of the fountain
in its fashion, the flowers among the well-colored
flowers, rustles in unison along the slippery river,
Then it is clear that
the peasant withdraws himself from those profits, both of them, I completely empty myself.
After mentioning these things, a certain one was speedily rowing,
with such a great length and distance of the road,
he reached the aforesaid town, weary, to the field,
where the pious lymph had been sold to the lord.
Not at once on foot, though curious,
He reaches the flowery threshold of the atrium,
He applies the fences near but from the palisade,
Nor not to the bristly briars and brambles,
Whose uncultivated sole was the roof on all sides,
Nor thorny feet tremble to desire.
Joining the precepts burning his fence lights,
To survey the glassy stream of water.
But still, moving forward, he looked with his eyes in vain,
because the source had completely ceased and was gone from here.
Then he turned his mind to the junctions ,
with his mind unable to see through the narrow clare of the hedge.
And when he sought the lake, and rebuked the bottom of the thirsty,
Who once luxuriated in strong waters,
Until the bed, empty hope not well played,
He began to lick the sandy places,
Trying if he could lick a little drop,
But he had not dyed a dry lick from here.
At last Gangolf felt
that the pious deeds of the chapel had been done.
After he had returned from here, he visited his comrades again,
He looked at the cloud, visible in the air,
Next to the sweet head of Christ to fly with hunger,
Like a white and fine shawl.
Catching him with his eyes, he began to denounce with the words
of the Fountain the failure, which he had learned, suddenly,
and he had urged his associates to put aside the doubt of their hearts,

and to become credulous by the merits of the saint.
In such conversations, while they speak words to their friends,
To apply themselves to their own lords,
Walls were made of flowers where they were built of locellus,
Around scattered trees of various kinds.
Here Christ's dear friend directed his step,
With his mind desiring to run through the court in purple,
And he carried the staff, which at last with nerves,
He fixed on the ground and soon went home.
There were innumerable wretched ministers in due order,
Present with various valiant duties,
Those who lay the tables laden with food,
Asking at last to relieve the late hunger.
But first he ordered the invalid crowd to proceed,
which he was accustomed to feed at the table many times with his own,
and, fully satisfied with his own hands,
At last he applied himself to the table placed before him.
The French, who had been thrown through the walls, sat down together,
tasting the berry gifts with joy.
In the meantime, the star urged him to sleep,
the night was approaching black and threatening darkness,
and the peaceful repast was suddenly followed by a friend,
creeping through his limbs, given to drunkenness.
The pious leader, sleepless,
began to spend the night praying to the Lord with his voice.
After the night had parted and departed, conquered by the darkness,
the rising light encircled the ethereal quarter,
The boys came, having won the lot of the servants,
Carrying the master's dear shoes,
And knocking in the hall, closed for the warmth of the night,
Praying that the entrance would now be made clear,
But the leader was silent for a while, and pretended to sleep,
Then, as if waking up from sleep with a pregnant woman,
he ordered the interior bars to be loosened,
and his dining room and soldiers to be spread out.
When these were introduced, he asked for the lymph with his white hands,
but at the Lord's nod he was absent from the throne.
Then the confident man, blessed by Christ's piety, quickly sent
one of the most excellent boys
to bring him the staff, remembered,
how late he fixed his own in the atrium.
Who, at a rapid pace, leaping through the grassy fields
Round his slippery and wandering eyes

Searching for the staff buried in the earth at the time,
And grasped with his fingers the nascent tree, And
pulled it out to the ground, a small remaining cave,
After this visible to make a label,
Certain by which a small cloud
fell before it was empty,
It vomited and the swellings were broken by the very cell,
The waves of the prescribed spring,
Mansuras also fixed the watery veins of the sledge,
The rod fixed where it was small.
But the boy was stunned, and his voice spread through the air.
Urging the soldiers to run faster,
he told them and the new ones the joys of the sign,
which the king of the army beckoned to the angelic ones.
He took one,
and filled it with lymph, which was quickly visible.
With a happy face, Gangolf also continued to the mountain,
so that he could tell himself an unusual sign.
And, standing before the consul with a serene countenance,
he spoke these words to the excellent man:
Happy, he said, you deservedly receive the rarest gifts,
which the earth did not bring you a little,
but the King himself of the poles, from the top of the sky,
sent a wonderful service through the clouds.
From this we are now able to take great joy,
You are so lucky because you are glorious.
Immediately, on the other hand, the leader, with a serene
mouth, gives such answers in a pious voice:
It is not worthy of these merits, he says,
it is enough to believe ours,
I have never received so much as nothing.
He had said, and, as usual, he dyed himself with the young fountain of
the Lotus, and from the high throne he sang these words to the Lord:
O ever piety, our only hope of life,
O power of the divine greatest grace!
You hate who you can is worthy to equal the work of the almighty
Artificer of the world to God,
Who gives new things to the past not inconsistent with the signs,
Who for generations through the ages rules his own.
These are the miracles proper to virtue, O Christ, who once
commanded the people, as the Jewish Rock, to pour out sweet milk,
and to make the salt of the sad lake sweet enough.
From there, I am not oblivious to the power of the thundering alma mater,

Which is the trinity of things by the right of the king,
This now and ours you wanted to believe in the earth,
The judgment of the great noble glory,
Wherein the inhabitants of the world may learn that
you are always alone, and were, God.
Now grant this also to the Lord Jesus, who prayed,
Let this liquid wash away the various diseases,
Where everyone praises you with sweet words,
Who feels himself saved and strong
Says these things, and the voice is followed by the soul speaking of salvation,
And the healthy water becomes, praise be to you, Lord.
After this, the machine of the world flying quickly through the vast expanses,
the betrayer of the sign, fame, quite pleased,
not only exhorts the countrymen, that is to say the colonists,
whose gifts happened to the goldsmith,
but also the faint-hearted strangers from afar,
gathered from all sides, to speed up quickly,
and to take the gifts of medicine at no cost
by tasting only a little spring.
More often you see the uncultivated crowd prostrate,
Rolling limbs on the languid shore,
So that you can believe that they are besieged by various diseases.
Adore the Jewish languid people,
Who once upon a time, in the arcades of Solomon's
Fus, the wall of the pool of Bethsaida,
They fought, the physician disturbing the lymph from above,
Who would wash away various diseases with a primrose,
Read such indeed wondrous under the lot,
That soon he slips away dishonored,
Many hanging in the light painfully following him,
Who for the hope of life are flaring greedily,
As a physician, suddenly slipping from the upper hinge,
Disturbed a little pond with his foot.
They desire nothing else, greedy of salvation,
To touch even the smallest drop of the spring,
And, having received the first taste of old health,
They throbbed with sweet starry ears,
Grateful for so much as a gift to Christ,
Who gave thanks to the poor for his holy merits.
With their praises they raise a man worthy above the air,
so much for his own sake that he holds good things.
If you have time, praise equal to merits,
And conduct so excellent a leader.

PASSION OF ST. GANGOLF

But leaving these things to the learned poets,
Let us paint the beginnings with a fragile pen.
Surely the people of the Franks, while laughing at Eous's
illustrious merits and goodness of the leader,
are flattered by the great prayers of the elders,
this dear of Christ, the nation and all the honor,
with whom he wished to associate a girl worthy of him by
a legal covenant, a customary marriage,
lest it should come to an end, carried away by posterity,
inclining the royal lineage of the race .
At last with these admonitions, Gangolf, the venerable leader,
touched by Sat, with flattering and paternal admonitions,
joined Ignis, a conspicuous friend of her own,
regal in race and fair in face.
He ordered her to always lead a liquid life,
combined with chaste behavior and studies.
To me he is but a covetous snake, cunning, bitter,
The temper of a married woman is immediately unteachable.
Of course, the unfortunate clerk of Gangolf was boldly
burning his own more lawful mistress.
Alas! these things, badly defeated by the bitter cunning of the serpent,
let the wretch heat up the sooner to the deed,
clinging to the servant, and with the secret warmth of his heart,
rejects the lawful master for the sake of the servant.
Then the savage scratched the enemy's crimes to expose them,
Which he thought had been built by his own trickery,
And impatient of delay, he threw them empty into the air,
Spreading his joy at last.
When it had been a thing that had been slandered by the common people,
the Frankish nation was pitiful to all the natives,
with the pulse of the thin tongues it was blown to the ears
of St. Gangolf, the consul of the Almifficus,
that he might take refuge, seeking, slipping through the narrow words,
not the least tidings of sorrow.
He groaned so sadly, the most deserving of wrongdoers,
He is touched by great anguish and a dart,
Inside the narrow chamber of the chest also rolls,
Different things for him, sad sorrowing, two;
Primula, to prepare revenge by the penal law,
For a crime so terrible a crime;
After that, I will love the forgiveness of the usual piety,
And it hurts for a time from here too much doubt.
Surely, at last, he paid the deserved

punishment in a pious way, He did not like to slander the crime any further,
He was only concerned to stop the wretched crime,
Nor after this should he live recklessly in crime.
And when the mind of pious care was loosed in them,
He happened to run through the atrium of his own,
Against the doors of the fountain which he himself had first sent,
Through the clouds through the strange heaven's office.
Here, where Gangolf himself had remained happy,
the lascivious Spouse had suddenly arrived.
As soon as the pacific words are spoken,
Talia dictating with a mouth quite pregnant: I
have learned from your side that your reputation is often left,
that you are a corrupt tore, if you own it.
I differ, but generally treat, pitying you,
until I know, perhaps, that you were not guilty.
Nor do I order a large crowd to gather together suddenly,
Incited by tears from all sides to the council,
That the senate, knowing the fine lot, Rolls
the cause, the terrible and the merit of the crime.
But I will advise you to dip your right hand only,
the frozen lymph of the present spring;
And if there is no sudden loss of what has happened, then
beyond judgment there is no need for another.
Whom then, more than just, trusting with a proud heart,
Comforting his hardness with the demon,
At last he commits the bare bottom to the palm,
Hoping that no harm can be done to him.
Burning among the cold, but he found the waves,
What could our lofty right hand of God do.
Of course, in the wet sand, the bold one burned,
He burns with the fierce flames of the equine,
And, which hates to yield to peaceable words,
Is forced to yield to eternal justice.
O, ever easy change of our Christ,
O, power of righteous judges equal to God!
For she who, by tossing, fancied herself in sorrowful sorrow,
Burns the dyed skin of her arm.
Nor did he delay, when he brought back the palm, which perhaps he denied,
He bore the crude evidence of the crime.
Having thus resolved upon these things, the mind, aware of the fraud, trembles,
beyond which there was no hope of pardon in life.
Only to be certain of death, and to be corrupted, and to be pardoned,

the punishment of Lethal was speedily inflicted.
But the sad merit of his mind had moderated his anger,
Prince Gangolf, an excellent judge,
Ordering that the cleric who was to be condemned
should be expelled suddenly from the country,
where the villain was venting his evil deeds.
But he is beaten by his country and given into exile,
And he gives the wretched pardon, pitying him,
with honor, He does not place him in a room beyond his own.
After this, Gangolf's fame growing blessed,
Laudatory of the life which was almifica, industrious
deceiver of men and captor of the guilty,
Evolving the old bile of envy,
Tried by frauds of all kinds of ancient cunning , to empty the good reputation,
Lest the nation, by such an example and so much urged,
Before his proud necks to the lord.
At that time he sweated for a long time with malicious fraud,
He was not able to injure the famous leader,
In the sun because the power of
His great love grew much more in the hearts of the people,
At last he surrounded the wretched with arms of fraud,
Whom, for the sake of crime,
he drove from his country,
he knew how to spare his master already.
Such a suffused suddenly with a wretched wretch,
To the death of the righteous and the pious,
And, recapturing Ganeas with malicious ferocity,
He laid bare to him all that he had studied.
The sooner these things, his wicked, alas! submitted to his vows,
He wished the deed to be done sooner,
He plans and plots just secretly to
do evil, Forgetful of the ancient, oh! penitent pardon,
With which he redeems himself from the punishment already duly prepared,
And does not suffer his life to perish by death.
With these the more ungrateful partner agreed with the unrighteous,
and the servile she-wolf burns with fire.
And when the night covered the pole with darkness, aware of the fraud,
He felt that the time was damning for the wolf,
How badly they can extinguish the holy Gangolf,
And this he tells the squire in a perverse way.
Who, cutting off the sacred thigh of
St. Gangolf, the great martyr,

fled with his bright spouse,
Raptured by the indomitable love of his mistress.
But as he did not know the legal end of love,
So he does not know that his revenge has a delay,
But suddenly the heavens spilled out their bowels, Spurred by
the joy of pride that had been swollen,
And thus the miserable, lofty prostrated with the right hand of the
avenger Life had lost Ganea.
For the holy martyr, wounded by a stealthy wound,
While he drank the taste of death fast,
Nor did he breathe his last dying breath in the hours,
An angelic group stood by,
With a voice that knew how to lay down a stable body as a witness,
Context with languid clay veins,
And no, gently caressed by angelic hymns,
Soon the paths of heaven to pick up the stars.
Expiring his soul quickly, the martyr, well bathed
in the bright purple blood of the Lamb,
is lifted from the air, and rides through the clear stars,
stands at the gate of heaven and the Lord.
Here a rare laurel is soon brought to him from Christ,
And in the hands of a brave man a perpetual palm,
And a shining robe is joined with white wedges
By the glad wound which the court holds the pole.
In the meantime the funeral is prepared with a great parade, and
They adorn the body and soul of the funeral.
All mourned the fall of so many patrons,
His servants were mostly but miserable,
and a place was chosen for the rich, venerating the mound,
which the old fathers handed down.
There Gangolf buried the members of the blessed,
scattering the sacred ashes with tears.
After this they not infrequently visited the sacred bones,
seeking a certain protection.
The bodies of the nobles are also spread with the bust,
for various causes of unsteady life.
As he who carries scepters, prostrated on the marble, licks,
and licks the marble mound with kisses.
Reflecting on the service, the hope, the words, with which the martyr's alms
for the merits of Christ may be more propitious to him.
What shall I report to the crowd of the temple thrown before the threshold,
or what shall I say of its countless wishes?
Surely no one can understand these things,

nor can any letters say them.
But on the other hand, the most successful witness
is given to them such a gift of sweetness.
Everyone feels that without delay everything will be successful.

Here surely the blind man, having recovered his sight,
soon draws bright lightnings from his eyes,
and ears long closed are opened by voices,
and the feet of the plants are restored to the invalids,
here also the sick are driven away from various diseases,
their limbs were cleansed and languishing at last.
I am not in a position to adequately advise the excellent
gifts that the people here are reaping.
And not only are the dear ones encouraged by the love of their patron,
whose citizens happen to be such men,
but also those who live in remote lands, perhaps,
feel the ready help of the martyr.
Hence, no land in the world boasts that it is happy,
Which embraces the sacred bones with its soft bosom.
Damnanda barathro,
Invita, appropriate to its own merits.
Certainly, when the victor's most joyous witness
The starry fame of the pole should pulsate, The entire
and stable borders of the world should traverse,
Spreading such glorious joys,
Rejoicing, devout, some man ran,
From the bust of signs composed of various signs,
Being met by the wolf, mentioned above,
He stopped, stunned looking with his eyes.
This one, too, for his merits, is related to
the words of the lover, conforming to his own words such as these:
Every unfortunate harlot to be believed in flames,
Is he now reluctant to fraud, repent or crime,
Into the sanctity of the Lord not prepared with a just mind,
Only partners in lascivious counsel?
For, taking pity on you, I spread the cosmetics
of the best plan, soon to be taken by you,
urging you to seek the sacred by deserving the grave,
Wipe away the stains and stains with tears,
There the soulless souls are holy because they have been buried as a witness.
And, though I am unworthy, I hope you will be
able to forgive me.
But the pestilence's mind, ill-given to all vices,

Refused to go the right way of life,
And now alone happily embracing the slippery life,
He cares not
for the perpetual joys of his country to have good deeds.
Of course, hearing the words of one who speaks no falsehood,
Turning his cunning bloodshot eyes, He shakes his untamed head impatiently at him
And barks with his beak such pestilence: the mound,
nothing else than the wonderful miracles of my back.
He had said, and the word is followed by a wonderful sign,
that proper particle.
Therefore he gave a sound, made with a vile melody,
As if our profaris were ashamed of such a song.
And after these words, as often as he had formed any,
he returned this uncultivated sound as often as not.
That which the law rejects to retain shame,
Let laughter be an immoderate cause for all, and
carry to the end of his life through the times of his life
the evidence of his own reproach.

LATIN TEXT

ARGUMENTUM IN GANGOLFUM.

Gangolfus, ex nobili Burgundiorum regum familia et sanguine natus, et in religione Christiana initiatus, a paupere quodam rustico hortulum, cum fonte amoenissimo, emerat, cujus amoenitatem Hrosvitha pulcherrime describit. In hunc hortulum, orationis et relaxationis animi gratia, dum ab armis et republica vacaret, solitus erat concedere, quam rem familiares sui vehementer oderant. Factum igitur est, ut fons exaruisset, quem ille, baculo in terram fixo, rursus largissima vena restituit, ita ut illius unda omnium morborum pestes, haurientium et lavantium fugaret. Tandem, uxorem ducens, quae incontinens et impudica fuerat, in amoreque satellitum suorum effrena libidine debacchata; quod cum sancto viro, Gangolfo, compertum fuisset, illam de incontinentia corripuit, illa per satellites insidias Gangolfo struxit, et ab illis interfectus, sepultus in loco, qui Nil terra dicitur, miraculis clarens. Quod cum relatum ad Ganeam, uxorem suam, fuisset, fidem miraculis ejus derogat, miraculaque non secus, ut ventris sui crepitum, existimat. Quamobrem in poenae perfidiam venter illi, quoad viveret, perpetuo crepabat.

PRAEFATIO IN GANGOLFUM.

O pie Lucisator, mundi rerumque Parator,
Qui coelum pingis sideribus variis,
Solus et astrigera regnans dominaris in aula
Lumine cuncta tenens, imperioque regens,
Tu, qui per proprium fecisti saecula Natum,
Et rerum trinam ex nihilo machinam,
Quique protoplasto, de terra rite creato,
Oris divini nectare nempe tui
Sensus vitalem sufflasti forte liquorem,
Ut fixum digiti fiat opus proprii,
Tu dignare tuae perfundere corda famellae,
Hrosvithae, rorentis pie gratiolae,
Carmine quo compto valeam pia pangere facta
Sancti Gangolfi, martyris egregii,
Et laudare tuum semper nomen benedictum,
Qui post bella tuis grata dabis famulis
Praemia, perspicuae tenui pro vulnere vitae,
Mandans in regno vivere lucifluo.

PASSIO SANCTI GANGOLFI MARTYRIS

Tempore quo regni gessit Pippinus Eoi
Francorum sceptra regia pro populo,
Jureque magnifico rexit Burgundia regna,
Subjectos frenis rite domando suis,
Famosus juvenis nutritur partibus illis,
Armis praevalidus, corpore conspicuus,
Nomine Gangolfus, morum probitate venustus,
Omnibus hic charus exstitit et placidus.
Illum nempe ferunt ortum de germine regum,
Regalemque suis moribus egregiis.
Ipsius e matris gremio spes pendet in illo,
Qui verbo cuncta condidit ex nihilo,
Germinis et tanti sese non credit honori,
Sed transit meritis stemma sui generis.
Inclyta nam genitrix, tali fetu pie felix,
In mundi lucem fudit ut hanc sobolem,
Ocius abluitur vetulis baptismate culpis,
Quas protoplastes obtinuere patres,
Chrismatis unguento scripto sibi fronteque signo,
Ascitur natis Ecclesiae nitidis,
Pascitur et plenae fidei mox dogmate trinae,
Dum vagit cuna corpore lacteolo.
Lac quotiens suxit, totiens fidei sacra sumpsit,
Suspensus matris uberibus geminis.
Talibus incubuit, lactis dum gurgite vixit,
Hinc pulsus, gravido ferbuit ingenio,
Canitiemque senum membris meditando tenellis,
Non raro sacris nempe vacat studiis.
Quem mox imberbem, tota probitate vigentem,
Gratia Pippini, principis almifici,
Regali non immerito sisti jubet aula,
Ardenter talem corde colens juvenem.

Sed pietas illum, quamvis justissima, regis,
Ditaret tantae munere gloriolae,
Regius ut primis esset proconsul ab annis,
Turgenti fastu non tamen erigitur,
Pectore sed tales humili fastidit honores,
Suspirans aulae munera sidereae.
Nam patrius census fuerat sibi maxime partus,
Dividit et tanto pauperibus studio,
Ceu Christum miseros inter sentiret egenos
Arridere suo munere fronte pio.
Saepe Job atque viri normam tractando beati,
Ipse manus manco, pes fuit et podagro,
Se nec non orbo cautum praebebat ocellum,
Exemplum cunctis nobile dans populis.
Nec minus humanis sudavit denique causis,
Aequalem primis se faciens dominis.
Nam, male si nostras aures simulata, vetustas
Non rebus fictis luserat, et dubiis,
Hic, quem nostra manus coepit jam pingere sanctus,
Est assuetus iter quadrupedum sequier,
Sedulo venando lassat quoque membra decora,
Succumbens charique imperio domini,
Ipsius et telum nunquam scit cedere victum,
Cum sint ferrati compositi cunei,
Effert ipse suum semper sed ab hoste triumphum,
Tutus divino coelitus auxilio.
Certe non nostrae possunt dictando Camenae
Composito modulis texere dactylicis,
Quantis dilectum signis variaverat istum
Rex regum, summa pro bonitate sua.
Sed tamen, inculto quamvis sermone, latrabo
Unum de claris pluribus et variis.
Ut res facta probat, turmas ducendo praeibat,
Capturus populum Marte satis tumidum,
Exstitit et solito victor mox denique bello,
Ejus non laeso sanguine purpureo,
Gentibus adversis juri proprioque subactis,

Censum signavit, pace data, rediit.
Contigit et, ducente via, se pergere, juxta
Cujusdam septa pauperis opposita,
Queis latuit pictum vernanti flore locellum,
Tectum multiplicis germinis atque comis,
Nec non fonticulus, vitreo candore serenus,
Profluxit, rivo rura rigans stridulo.
Huc ubi praeclarus senior deduxit ocellos,
Perlustrans liquidam fonticuli scatebram,
Frigoreae captus lymphae paulisper amore,
Substitit, et placitis tardat iter morulis,
Et mittens puerum, venisse rogabat ad illum
Florigeri dominum ipsius ergo loci.
Qui praecepta ducis complens extemplo jubentis,
Quo fuerat jussus, egreditur citius.
Hunc dux ipse quidem dum respexit venientem,
Aggreditur blandis protinus alloquiis,
Atque rogans humilis tota dulcedine mentis,
Formavit lingua talia verba sua:
Dulcis amice, meis precibus sis, postulo, largus,
Ut vendas purum hunc mihi fonticulum,
Qui, clarus vitreis et suave sonantibus undis,
Prolambens arva haec irrigat atque tua,
Et mox argenti tibi pro mercede probati
Largiter infundo pondera non modica.
Ast ubi, tinnitum dando, promissio laeta
Aures personae transit in exiguae,
Laetatur facies, totae volitant quoque venae,
Cordis secreto quae latuere loco.
Tunc miser in talem coepit prorumpere vocem.
Ultra quam credas, spem dubiamque sciens,
O nostrate decus, nulli pietate secundus,
Quem colit Eous mente, fide, populus,
Qui tibi, quid digni potis est mea lingula fari?
Nonne tuis manibus est sita nostra salus?
Et quidquid mihi per verbum sancis faciendum,
Quamvis difficile sit satis atque grave,

Attamen est aequum tibi me parere, beate,
Ut dudum summo me exiguum domino.
Si placet hinc vetulum me transmigrare colonum,
Non contraluctor, sed tua jussa sequor.
Haec ait, et pressis frenat sua verbula labris,
Nec post verbosa quid sequitur ligula.
Et contra vir regalis pie talia fantis
Suscepit dicta pro bonitate sua,
Et citius dicto solvit promissa misello,
Illi centenos attribuens solidos.
Haec ubi perfecit, raptim redeundo migravit,
Nitens ad patriam pergere posthabitam.
Tunc, qui non gnari fuerant signi venerandi,
Olim facturus quod fuit Altithronus,
Blasphemare ducem tacitis coepere susurris,
Et pietatis opus spernere ceu facinus.
Credito, non latuisse dolum pietatis homullum,
Sed mox nudari clancula dicta sibi.
Qui dedit arguto vocem tunc nempe palato,
His verbisque suos alloquitur socios,
Cur libet, o socii, vosmet reprendere, chari,
Plus justo, verbis me satis illicitis?
Causa stultitiae, dicentes, me tribuisse,
Ignoto nummos extraneoque viro,
Me vacuum tanti meritoque dolere locelli,
Et bene a me mercati utpote fonticuli,
Dextera ceu propria census est, quae pie larga,
Aurum pro donis si dederim minimis.
Non decet hoc nostris vobis reserarier orsis,
Quid velit addicti causa sibi pretii,
Mentes sed motas praestat componere vestras,
Et rogo parcatis talibus alloquiis,
E vobisque virum caute nunc credite gnarum,
Emissis ventis aeribusque vagis,
Ut jam semotum citius repetendo locellum
Lustret, sit vena fonticuli liquida
More suo, flores inter bene multicolores

Perstrepet, undisono flumine per lubrica,
Tunc patet, ille lucris sese subtractat ab illis
Rusticus, ambobus, me vacuo penitus.
Haec postquam memorat, cursim quidam remeabat,
Tantae dimenso atque viae spatio,
Oppido praedictum lassus pervenit ad arvum,
Quo fuerat domino vendita lympha pio.
Non tamen extemplo pedibus, quamvis curiosus
Attigit atrioli limina florigeri,
Applicat impexis juxta sed de paliuris,
Nec non hirsutis vepribus et tribulis,
Queis fuit incultum soli torus undique tectum,
Nec spineta pede horruit appetere.
Jungere praescriptis ardens sua lumina septis,
Ut lustraret aquae amniculum vitreae.
Sed tamen admotis frustra prospexit ocellis,
Fons quia desierat prorsus et hinc aberat.
Tunc se juncturas volvebat mente per arcta
Clare non posse cernere sepiculae,
Ac tractim rigida, nec non cervice superba,
Incedens, gressus vertit in atriolum,
Sperans sub foliis quod forte lateret amoenis
Florum multimodis undula tecta comis.
Cumque lacum peteret, fundumque siti reprobaret
Qui quondam validis luxuriavit aquis,
Usque solum stratus, vacua spe non bene lusus,
Coepit arenosa lingere nempe loca,
Tentans exiguam posset si lambere guttam,
Sed nec praesiccam tinxerat hinc ligulam.
Tandem Gangolphi sensit pia facta sacelli
Sed dolet et meritis credere nolle piis.
Hinc postquam rediit, socios iterumque revisit,
Aspexit nubem, aere conspicuam,
Juxta dulce caput Christi volitare famelli,
Instar candiduli denique pallioli.
Hanc capiens oculis, coepit depromere verbis
Fontis defectum, quem didicit, subitum,

Suaserat et sociis, dubium deponere cordis,
Et meritis sancti jam credulos fieri.
Talia colloquiis dum verba loquuntur amicis,
Applicuere sui in propriis domini,
Moenia florigero fuerant ubi structa locello,
Circum diffusis arboribus variis.
Hic Christi charus gressum direxit amicus,
Mente libens atrio currere purpureo,
Et baculum, tractis gessit quem denique nervis,
In terram fixit moxque domum petiit.
Illic innumeri certabant rite ministri,
Instantes variis fortiter officiis,
Ipsi qui mensas dapibus ponunt oneratas,
Poscentes tandem solvere sero famem.
Sed prius invalidam jussit procedere turbam,
Quam suevit mensa pascere saepe sua,
Ac, propriis ipsa manibus plene saturata,
Se tandem mensa applicat apposita.
Accumbunt pariter Franci per moenia fusi,
Gustantes bacchica munera laetitia.
Interea somnum sidus suadebat Eoum,
Nox vicina nigras et minitat tenebras,
Atque quies epulas subito sequebatur amica,
Serpens per membra, ebrietate data.
Dux pius insomnem coepit transducere noctem,
Intenta Dominum voce precando suum.
Postquam nox scissis discessit victa tenebris,
Lux orta plagam cinxerat aetheream,
Venerunt pueri, tironum sorte potiti,
Portantes chari calceolos domini,
Et pulsant aulam, noctis pro tepore clausam,
Orantes, aditum jam fieri patulum,
Sed dux paulisper siluit, somnum quoque finxit,
Post, velut e somno evigilans gravido,
Solvere custodi vectes jubet interiores,
Pandere triclinium militibusque suum.
His introductis, lympham manibus petit albis,

Sed nutu Domini defuit altithroni.
Tunc vir securus, Christi pietate beatus,
Unum de pueris ocius egregiis,
Ut sibi deferret virgam, misit, memoratam,
Quam sero proprium fixit in atriolum.
Qui, cursu rapido, saliendo per herbida rura
Circumfert lubricos atque vagos oculos
Inquirens baculum terrae tempore sepultum,
Et nactum tractis arripuit digitis,
Extraxitque solo, parva remanente caverna,
Post haec conspicuum ut faceret titulum,
Certo quo facto cecidit nubecula parva,
Quae volitans aura ante fuit vacua,
Evomit et tumidas ipso disrupta locello,
Undas praescripti denique fonticuli,
Mansuras scatebrae venas quoque fixit aquosae,
Virgula praefixa quo fuit exigua.
At puer obstupuit, vocemque per aera spargit.
Suadens militibus currere jam citius,
Illis atque novi narravit gaudia signi,
Quae rex militiae annuit angelicae,
Dum subito cuncti, tanto signo tremefacti,
Tollunt mirantes ad superos facies,
Expassisque suis omnes ad sidera palmis,
Laudum carminula concinuere Deo,
Ecce, palatinus pelvem manibus tulit unus,
Implevit lympha quem cito conspicua,
Laeto Gangolfum vultu quoque pergit ad almum,
Ut sibimet signum diceret insolitum.
Et, coram tanto subsistens fronte serena
Consule, de rostro haec dedit egregio:
Laetus, ait, merito sumas rarissima dona,
Quae tibi non terra contulit exigua,
Sed Rex ipse poli, summo de vertice coeli,
Per nubis mirum miserat officium.
Hinc nos laetitiam constat nunc carpere magnam,
Sortitus tantam es quia gloriolam.

Illicet e contra fatur dux ore sereno
Reddens responsa talia voce pia:
Non decet his meritis, inquit, sat credere nostris,
Unquam tantilli nil quia commerui,
Restat multiplices Christo sed pangere grates,
Qui praesens famulis semper adest propriis.
Dixerat, et solito tinxit se fonte novello
Lotus, et altithrono haec cecinit Domino:
O semper pietas nostrae spes unica vitae,
O vis divinae maxima gratiolae!
Odis quis potis est dignis opus omnipotentis
Artificis mundi aequiparare Dei
Qui nova praeteritis reddit non dissona signis,
Qui nam per genitum saecla regens proprium.
Haec sunt virtutis propriae miracula, Christe,
Qui quondam populo utpote Judaico
Petram jussisti lactes effundere dulces,
Et sal triste laci dulce satis fieri.
Inde, potestatis non immemor alme Tonantis
Qua rerum trinam jure regis machinam,
Hoc nunc et nostris voluisti credere terris,
Judicium magnae nobile gloriolae,
Quo discant teretem degentes saepe per orbem,
Te semper solum esse, fuisse, Deum.
Hoc quoque nunc Jesu Domino concede precatu,
Abluat ut morbos iste liquor varios,
Quo te dulcisonis collaudet vocibus omnis,
Qui se salvatum sentiat et validum
Haec ait, et vocem sequitur salus alma loquentem,
Fitque salubris aqua, laus tibi sit Domino.
Post haec, pervasti volitans cito machina mundi,
Proditrix signi, fama, satis placiti,
Non solum patrios hortatur nempe colonos,
Queis fungi dono contigit aurivago,
Sed quoque languidulos de longinquo peregrinos,
Undique collectos, accelerare citos,
Et nullo pretio medicinae sumere dona

Gustando tantum fonticuli modicum.
Crebrius incultam videas procumbere turbam
Volventem membra littore languidula,
Ut possis variis obsessos credere morbis
Adfore Judaici languidulos populi,
Qui quondam quivis, in porticibus Salomonis
Fusi, piscinae obice Bethsaidae,
Certabant, medico lympham turbante superno,
Primule quis morbos ablueret varios,
Lege quidem tali mira sub sorte potiti,
Ut mox illapsus exueret dedecus,
Pluribus in lucem suspensis aegre sequentem,
Qui pro spe vitae efflagitant avidae,
Ut raptim medicus, supero de cardine lapsus,
Turbaret modicam vel pede piscinulam.
Haud alias isti cupiere, salutis avari,
Tangere vel guttam fonticuli minimam,
Et, gustu primo veteri sanitate recepta,
Pulsabant odis sidera dulcisonis,
Grates pro tanto reddentes munere Christo,
Qui sancti meritis grata dedit miseris.
Laudibus aeque virum tollunt super aethera dignum,
Tanta sui causa quod tenuere bona.
Si vacet, aequales meritis protendere laudes,
Et mores tanti egregios duculi
Ante dies noctis peplo velatur olympo,
Quam metam nostra obtineat ratio.
Haec sed linquentes doctis tractanda poetis,
Pingamus coepta nos fragili calamo.
Certe Francorum populus dum risit Eous
Illustris meritis et bonitate ducis,
Blanditur magnis procerum precibus seniorum,
Hic Christi charus, gentis et omne decus,
Quo sibi condignam vellet sociare puellam
Foedere legali, conjugii soliti,
Ne finem caperet, subducta posteritate,
Inclyta regalis prosapies generis.

His tandem monitis Gangolfus, dux venerandus,
Sat tactus, blandis atque patrum monitis,
Igni conspicuam proprio jungebat amicam,
Regalem genere et nitidam facie.
Hanc jussit liquidam semper deducere vitam,
Compositam castis moribus et studiis.
Ei mihi, sed coluber cupidus, versutus, amarus,
Ingenium nuptae illicet indocile.
Scilicet infelix Gangolfi clericus audax
Ardebat propriam plus licito dominam.
Proh dolor! haec, male victa dolo serpentis amaro
Infelix citius aestuat in facinus,
Inhaerens servo, cordisque calore secreto
Legalem dominum respuit ob famulum.
Crimina tunc hostis scalpsit nudare feralis,
Quae caluit proprio structa fuisse dolo,
Impatiensque morae, vacuas jaculabat in auras,
Divulgando suam denique laetitiam.
Cum fuerat vulgo res diffamata dolenda,
Francorum gentis omnibus indigenis,
Pulsu linguarum tenues conflatur ad aures
Sancti Gangolfi, consulis almifici,
Ut capiat latebras, poscens, illapsa per arctas
Verbula, non minimae nuntia moestitiae.
Ingemuit tam triste nefas dignissimus beros,
Angoris magno tangitur et jaculo,
Intus in angusto volvit quoque pectoris aula,
Res sibi diversas, triste dolendo, duas;
Primule, vindictam poenali lege parandam,
Pro sceleris tanti crimine terribili;
Post vero, veniam solitae pietatis amandam,
Et dolet ad tempus hinc nimium dubius.
Certe sed meritam solvit tandem pie poenam,
Diffamare scelus nec placet ulterius,
Sollicitus tantum miserae crimen prohibere,
Nec post haec temere viveret in scelere.
Cumque piam curis mentem laxaret in illis,

Contigit atriolo currere se proprio,
Contra fonticuli sibimet prius ostia missi,
Nubis per mirum coelitus officium.
Hic ubi Gangolfus subsisteret ipse beatus,
Conjux lasciva adfuerat subito.
Quam mox pacificis affatur denique verbis,
Talia dictando ore satis gravido:
Parte tuam famam didici persaepe sinistram,
Quod corrupta toro sis male si proprio.
Differo sed vulgo tractare, tui miserando,
Donec forte sciam, te ne fuisse ream.
Nec mando, multam subito concurrere turbam,
Accitam flendo undique concilio,
Ut volvat gnarus subtili sorte senatus,
Causam, terribilis et meritum sceleris.
Sed suadebo manum dextram te tingere tantum,
Praesentis lympha fonticuli gelida;
Et, si non subito damni quid contigit, ergo
Ultra judicio non opus est alio.
Quem tunc, plus justo, confidens corde superbo,
Confortante suam daemone duritiam,
Fundo nudatam committit denique palmam,
Nil sperans damni posse sibi fieri.
Inter frigoreas ardens sed comperit undas,
Quid posset nostri dextera celsa Dei.
Scilicet in madidis audax ardebat arenis,
Uritur et flammis acriter aequoreis,
Et, quae pacificis fastidit cedere verbis,
Cogitur aeternae cedere justitiae.
O, semper nostri facilis mutatio Christi,
O, virtus justi judicis aequa Dei!
Nam, quae jactando finxit se triste dolendo,
Exuritur tincti pellicula brachii.
Nec mora, cum palmam retulit, quod forte negavit,
Portavit crudum criminis indicium.
His ita digestis, pavitat mens conscia fraudis,
Ultra nec vitae spes fuerat veniae.

Tantum certa mori, corruptelamque piari,
Lethali poena ocius apposita.
Sed tristis meritam mentis mitigaverat iram,
Princeps Gangolfus, arbiter egregius,
Mandans, ut propria damnandus clericus ergo
Expulsus subito pergeret e patria,
Quo sua finetenus mala defleret scelerosus.
Sed pulsus patria est et datus exsilio,
Et donat miseram veniae, miseratus, honore,
Ultra sed proprio non locat in thalamo.
Post haec, Gangolfi fama crescente beati,
Laudatrix vitae quae fuit almificae,
Vafer deceptor hominum captorque reorum,
Evolvens bilem invidiae veterem,
Fraudibus omnigenis antiquae calliditatis
Tentavit, famam evacuare bonam,
Ne gens, exemplo tali tantoque suasa,
Ante superba sua colla daret domino.
Tempore tunc longo sudavit fraude maligna,
Laedere famosum nec valuit duculum,
In soles quia multo magis vis crevit amoris
Illius magni cordibus in populi,
Postremo fraudis miserum circumdedit armis,
Quem, sceleris causa, reppulit e patria,
Sanguinis huncque siti jussit fervere superbi,
Nec scivit proprio parcere jam domino.
Tali suffusus subito cum felle misellus,
In mortem justi aestuat atque pii,
Ac, parili repetens Ganeam feritate malignam,
Illi nudavit omnia quae studuit.
Ocius haec, ejus pravis, heu! subdita votis,
Optavit, citius jam fieri facinus,
Tendit et insidias justo clam nempe nefandas,
Immemor antiquae, vah! penitus veniae,
Qua se de poena solvit jam rite paranda,
Nec patitur vitam morte perire ream.
His ingrata magis socio consensit iniquo,

Servilique lupa uritur igniculo.
Cumque polum tegeret tenebris nox conscia fraudis,
Sensit damnanda tempus inesse lupa,
Quo male Gangolfum possunt exstinguere sanctum,
Haec et perverso nuntiat armigero.
Qui, resecans coxam stricto mucrone sacratam,
Sancti Gangolfi, martyris eximii,
Deseruit patriam, fugiens cum conjuge, claram,
Raptus amore suae indomito dominae.
Sed non legalis finem ut nescivit amoris,
Sic vindicta suam nescit habere moram,
Viscera sed subito profudit coelitus, acta
Pridem laetitia quae fuerant tumida,
Sicque miser, celsa prostratus vindice dextra
Vita mercatam perdiderat Ganeam.
Nam martyr sanctus, furtivo vulnere laesus,
Dum mortis gustum ebiberet rapidum,
Nec non supremis moriens spiraret in horis,
Astabat coetus cominus angelicus,
Voce ciens stabilem corpus deponere testem,
Contextum venis fictile languidulis,
Nec non, angelicis blanditum suaviter hymnis,
Mox coeli calles carpere sidereas.
Ocius exspirans animam, martyr, bene lotam
Agni lucenti sanguine purpurei,
Tollitur ex aura, vehiturque per astra serena,
In coeli porta sistitur et Domino.
Hic sibi de Christo fertur mox laurea rara,
Et manibus bravii palmula perpetui,
Lucentique stola cuneis conjungitur albis
Per vulnus laeti quos tenet aula poli.
Funeris interea magni fit pompa parati,
Ornant exsequiae corpus et exanime.
Plangebant cuncti casum tantique patroni,
Ipsius famuli maxime sed miseri,
Eligiturque locus tumulo locuples venerando,
Quem tradunt veteres Nil vocitare patres.

Illic Gangolfi condebant membra beati,
Sacros spargentes cum lacrymis cineres.
Post haec non raro visitabant ossa sacrata,
Quaerentes certum denique praesidium.
Sternuntur sacro procerum quoque corpora busto,
Pro vitae causis instabilis variis.
Ast qui sceptra gerit, prostratus marmore, lambit,
Et libat tumulo oscula marmoreo.
Munere, spe, dictis recogitans, quo martyris almi
Pro meritis Christus sit sibi propitius.
Quid referam turbam templi pro limine jactam,
Quidve loquor vota illius innumera?
Haec certe nullus potis est comprendere sensus,
Nec possunt ullae dicere litterulae.
At contra vero testis prosperrimus ipsis
Largitur talis munera dulcedinis,
Omnis ut absque mora sentit, fore prospera cuncta,
Efflagitant testem pro quibus egregium.
Hic certe laeto caecis visu reparato,
Haurit mox oculis fulmina clara suis,
Atque diu clausae reserantur vocibus aures,
Et gressus plantis redditur invalidis,
Hic quoque de variis morbus depellitur aegris,
Mundatis membris denique languidulis.
Orsis non valeo digne praeclara monere
Munera, quae populus hic metit egregius.
Nec solum chari refoventur amore patroni,
Queis cives tanti contigit esse viri,
Sed pariter terris habitantes forte remotis,
Sentiscunt promptum martyris auxilium.
Hinc se felicem jactat Nil terra per orbem,
Quae molli gremio confovet ossa sacra,
Denique summatim, coepi quia tangere sancti
Gangolfi facta, martyris, egregia,
Restat, ut et tenui repetam sermone misellam,
Illius indignam conjugio, Ganeam,
Quodque dedit signum, merito damnanda barathro,

Invita, propriis conveniens meritis.
Certe, victoris cum jam laetissima testis
  Pulsaret celsi sidera fama poli,
Totos et stabilis fines percurreret orbis,
  Divulgans tantae gaudia gloriolae,
Gaudens, devotus, quidam currebat homullus,
  E busto signis composito variis,
Obvius atque lupae factus, supra memoratae,
  Substitit, attonitis aspiciens oculis.
Hanc quoque, pro meritis, dictis affatur amaris,
  Conformans ligula talia verba sua:
Omnis infelix flammis credenda meretrix,
  Jamne piget fraudis, poenitet aut sceleris,
In sanctum Domini non justa mente parati,
  Solo lascivi consilio socii?
Nam, miserando tui, pando medicamina sani
  Optima consilii, mox capienda tibi,
Suadens ut sacrum quaeras merendo sepulcrum,
  Abstergas fusis et maculas lacrymis,
Illic exanimis sancte quia condita testis
  Praefulgent signis fragmina non minimis.
Et, licet indignam, spero te posse misellam,
  Si defles culpam, consequier veniam.
Pestiferis sed mens vitiis male dedita totis,
  Ad vitae rectam rennuit ire viam,
Solaque nunc laetae complectens lubrica vitae,
  Non curat patriae gaudia perpetuae
Si haec infelix, commissi criminis auctrix,
  Fastidit verbis cedere pacificis,
Se quia credebat causis totam perituris,
  Nec spem mansuris gestit habere bonis.
Scilicet, auditis verbis non falsa loquentis,
  Intorquens oculos subdola sanguineos,
Exagitat caput indomitum impatienter in illum
  Et latrat rostro talia pestifero:
Cur loqueris, frustra simulans miracula tanta
  Sedulo Gangolfi pro meritis fieri

Haec quae dicuntur certe non vera probantur,
Non desint signa illius ut tumulo,
Haud alias quam mira mei miracula dorsi
Proferat extrema denique particula.
Dixerat, et verbum sequitur mirabile signum,
Illi particulae conveniens propriae.
Ergo dedit sonitum, turpi modulamine factum,
Profari nostram quale pudet ligulam.
Et post haec verbum quoties formaverat ullum,
Reddidit incultum hunc toties sonitum.
Ut quae legalem respuit retinere pudorem,
Sit risus causa omnibus immodica,
Finitenusque suae portet per tempora vitae
Indicium proprii scilicet opprobrii.

The Scriptorium Project is the work of a small group of lay people of various apostolic churches who are interested in the preservation, transmission, and translation of the works of the early and medieval church. Our efforts are to make the works of the church fathers accessible to anyone who might have an interest in Christian antiquities and the theological, philosophical, and moral writings that have become the bedrock of Western Civilization.

To-date, our releases have pulled from the Greek, Syriac, Georgian, Latin, Celtic, Ethiopian, and Coptic traditions of Christianity, and have been pulled from sundry local traditions and languages.

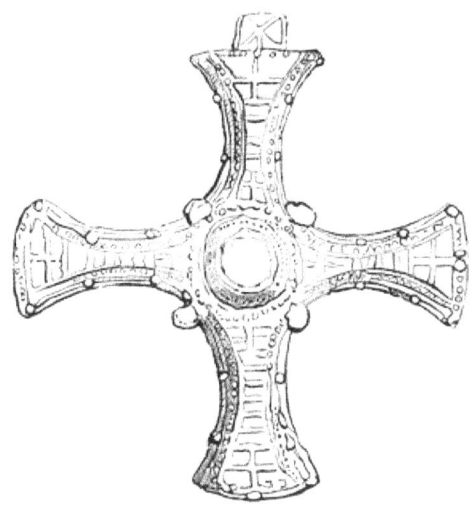

Other Selections from the Medieval German Church Series:

Passion of St. Gangolf by Hrotsvitha of Gandersheim (Oct. 2005)
Acts of the Synod of Ingelheim by Otto I, Holy Roman Emperor (Nov. 2005)
Church Documents by Louis II the German (Dec. 2005)
Paphnutius & Thaïs by Hrotsvitha of Gandersheim (June 2011)
Letters by Rudolf I Habsburg, Holy Roman Emperor (Dec. 2012)
About Fifteen Problems (De quindecim problematibus) by St. Albertus Magnus (Feb 2022)
On Fate (De Fato) by St. Albertus Magnus (Feb 2023)

www.ingramcontent.com/pod-product-compliance
Lightning Source LLC
LaVergne TN
LVHW061042070526
838201LV00073B/5154